BLACK HISTORY MAKERS

Rulers and Leaders

Adam Sutherland

Black History Makers: Rulers and Leaders is an introduction to some of black history's most prominent world leaders, all of whom have successfully brought about change. These rulers and leaders, with the backing of friends, families and their supporters, have proven time and again that with enormous courage and strength, anything is within reach.

All of the rulers and leaders in this book, whether they are from the past or are the rulers of today, have remained true to their beliefs, political opinions and faith, even while they have been shot at, publicly ridiculed or imprisoned for speaking out and fighting for what they believe in.

The strength of these rulers and leaders, coupled with the legacies they leave behind can inspire all of us to stand up for our opinions and beliefs so that maybe, one day, we can take up the mantle ourselves and in our own way become great and inspirational leaders, too.

Published in paperback in 2014 by Wayland
Copyright © Wayland 2014

Wayland
Hachette Children's Books
338 Euston Road
London NW1 3BH

Wayland Australia
Level 17/207 Kent Street
Sydney, NSW 2000

All rights reserved.
Editor: Katie Woolley
Designer: Tim Mayer, MayerMedia
Consultant: Mia Morris OBE, Black History Month website

British Library Cataloguing in Publication Data
Sutherland, Adam.
  Rulers and leaders. -- (Black history makers)
  1. Blacks--Politics and government--Juvenile literature.
  2. Blacks--History--Juvenile literature. 3. Kings and
  rulers--Biography--Juvenile literature.
  I. Title II. Series
  909'.0496-dc22

ISBN: 978 0 7502 8858 3

Printed in China

10 9 8 7 6 5 4 3 2 1

Wayland is a division of Hachette Children's Books,
an Hachette UK company. www.hachette.co.uk

Picture acknowledgements
Back Page Images/Rex Features: 23TC, Neilson Barnard/Getty Images: 23TR, Orlando Barria/EFE/Corbis: 17, Bettmann/Corbis: 5, William Campbell/Sygma/Corbis: 12, Don Hogan Charles/New York Times Co./Getty Images: 15, Mary Evans Picture Library: 6, Bru Garcia/AFP/Getty Images: 19, Hulton Archive/Getty Images: 8, Hulton-Deutsch Collection/Corbis: 4, Alexander Joe/AFP/Getty Images: 3, 11 Alisdair Macdonald/Rex Features: 23BR, W.Robert Moore/National Geographic Society/Corbis: 9, Photoshot: 13, Jason Reed/Reuters/Corbis: 18, Shutterstock Images: Cover, Title page, 7, 16, 20, 21, 23BC, 23TL, Siphiwe Sibeko/Reuters/Corbis: 10, Leif Skoogfors/Corbis: 14, c. 2004 TopFoto/UPP/TopFoto.co.uk: 23BL

CONTENTS

Words in **bold** can be found in the glossary on page 24.

Making History

From the sixteenth to the nineteenth centuries, millions of Africans were transported from west and central Africa to work as slaves all over the world. Many were sent to work on **plantations** in the south of the United States of America (USA) and on the islands of the Caribbean.

Many people opposed this slavery and it was fought around the globe. Leaders like Queen Nzinga in Angola (page 6) and Toussaint Louverture in Haiti (page 7) fought not only to end slavery but also to try to earn their countries' freedom.

Nineteenth century Abyssinian slaves held in chains, before being sold at a slave market.

In a protest against **segregation** in South Africa, these South African people have taken over a train compartment marked 'For Europeans Only'.

African independence

Between the 1880s and the start of the First World War in 1914, much of Africa was taken over and ruled by European countries. Up until the 1950s and 1960s, white **minorities** controlled African governments. These European **colonisers** would sell a country's natural resources like copper, cotton, rubber and cocoa and keep the profit for themselves.

Kenneth Kaunda (page 12) helped Zambia escape this colonial rule and established a well-governed country with an outstanding education system. When Kaunda came to power in 1964 there were 100 university graduates in Zambia. By the time he retired in 1991 there were 12,000!

Fighting apartheid

In 1948, the National Party was elected in South Africa, bringing with it their policy of **apartheid**, a system of legalised **racial discrimination**. The black **majority** in the country were forced to live in certain areas, work in certain jobs, study at certain schools and even eat in certain restaurants that the government decided were suitable.

Nelson Mandela (page 10) battled the white apartheid government, spending 27 years in prison for fighting this unfair system. As a free man, he helped to end apartheid and became South Africa's first **democratically elected** President.

While these rulers and leaders have lived and ruled across the world, they have all worked for freedom, independence and the well-being of their fellow men and women.

Queen Nzinga
Freedom Fighter

In the sixteenth century, Portuguese slave traders set up camp in Congo and South West Africa. They stole land from the locals to build their bases, captured men, women and children to work and sell as slaves and employed 'mercenaries' (professional soldiers, from the Imbangala tribe) to stop resistance from local forces. The person who led the fiercest opposition to the Portuguese and their mercenaries was Queen Nzinga.

Name: Nzinga Mbande

Born: circa 1583, Costa de Caparique, Angola

Died: 17 December 1663

Position: Queen of the Ndongo and Matamba Kingdoms of the Mbundu tribes in South West Africa (later Angola)

Awards and achievements: Brought peace to Angola, resettled former slaves and united her country.

Interesting fact: When she first met the Portuguese governor, Nzinga used one of her handmaidens as her 'seat' rather than take an inferior, standing position.

Queen Nzinga is still remembered in Angola for her intelligence, political skills and brilliant military tactics.

Going into battle

In 1622, Nzinga's brother Ngola Mbandi tried to get these slave traders to stop fighting against local forces and to release many of the slaves they held. The Portuguese agreed but soon broke their promises. When Ngola committed suicide in despair, Nzinga took his place as ruler of the Mbundu people and took the title of Queen of Andongo.

Nzinga's legacy

Nzinga declared war against the Portuguese in 1624, eventually forcing Portugal to sign a **peace treaty** in 1657. This allowed Nzinga to focus on rebuilding her war-damaged country and resettling former slaves. She died peacefully in 1663 at the age of 80.

Toussaint Louverture
Revolutionary Leader

Toussaint Louverture was a former slave who worked on one of Haiti's plantations before being freed at the age of 33. He was determined to end slavery in Haiti and led **guerrilla troops** into battle against British, Spanish and French forces many times. He took control of Haiti in 1801, **abolished** slavery and became Haiti's leader.

Imprisonment

The French President Napoleon Bonaparte sent troops to regain control of Haiti in 1802. Louverture signed a peace treaty with France but the French falsely accused him of plotting against Napoleon.

Name: Francois-Dominique Toussaint Louverture

Born: 20 May 1743, Breda, Haiti

Died: 7 April 1803

Position: Leader of the Haitian Revolution, 1791–1803

Awards and achievements: Abolished slavery and secured Haitian control of the colony.

Interesting fact: English poet William Wordsworth wrote a poem about Louverture in 1803 called To Toussaint L'Ouverture.

Louverture was arrested and taken to France where he died in prison in 1803. Six months after regaining control of Haiti, Napoleon decided to concentrate on his Empire in Europe and gave Haiti back its independence.

Toussaint Louverture was a slave who worked as a driver and horse trainer before being freed.

MAKING HISTORY

Toussaint Louverture was the leader of the first ever successful slave **revolution**. Through his efforts, Haiti became the first free black **republic** in the world when it declared independence on 1 January 1804.

Haile Selassie
The African Moderniser

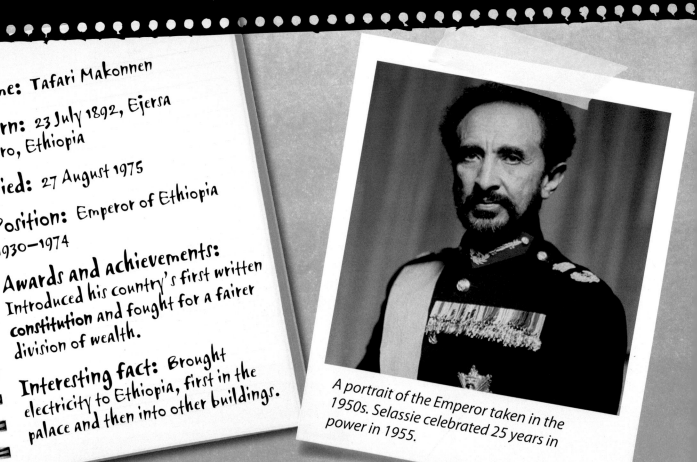

Name: Tafari Makonnen

Born: 23 July 1892, Ejersa Goro, Ethiopia

Died: 27 August 1975

Position: Emperor of Ethiopia 1930–1974

Awards and achievements: Introduced his country's first written constitution and fought for a fairer division of wealth.

Interesting fact: Brought electricity to Ethiopia, first in the palace and then into other buildings.

A portrait of the Emperor taken in the 1950s. Selassie celebrated 25 years in power in 1955.

A royal heir

Haile Selassie was born Tafari Makonnen. The heir to an Ethiopian royal family, his mother was daughter of the ruler of the Wollo province and his father the governor of Harar. His father died in 1906 when Selassie was 14 years of age and the young man immediately inherited control of Selale and Sidamo provinces. Over the next few years Selassie's experience and influence grew and when Empress Zewditu died in 1930, he was crowned Emperor of Ethiopia.

In power

As soon as he became Emperor, Selassie set out to make his country a better governed and fairer country than it had been in the past. He introduced the first written constitution in 1931, which saw **democratic** rule in the country for the first time. Unfortunately, his efforts were put on hold when Italy invaded Ethiopia and, in May 1936, Selassie and his family were forced into **exile**. He returned home when his country was liberated in 1941.

Haile Selassie and Queen Menen pose in their robes in 1931, not long after he was crowned Emperor in November 1930.

Lasting legacy

After the Second World War (1939–1945), Ethiopia became a **founder member** of the United Nations (UN). A modern, forward-thinking ruler, Selassie fought for a fairer division of land and wealth in his country. His planned **economic reforms** met with strong opposition from the country's landowners but he never stopped trying.

The end of his reign

During celebrations for his 25 years in power in 1955, he unveiled a revised constitution. A fully democratic system of voting was introduced, along with modern education methods. Selassie was eventually forced from power in September 1974 and died in August 1975.

Nelson Mandela
The Symbol of Hope

Nelson Mandela's grandfather was king of the Thembu people and his father was chief of the town of Mvezo. The young Mandela was the first in his family to receive an education and he started a degree at Fort Hare University. However, Nelson was asked to leave less than two years later because he was involved in a student protest against racist university selection policies. He started work at a Johannesburg law firm instead and completed his degree by **correspondence course**.

Name: Nelson Rolihlahla Mandela

Born: 18 July 1918, Mvezo, South Africa

Died: 5 December 2013

Position: President of South Africa 1994–1999

Awards and achievements: The first South African President to be elected in a fully democratic election.

Interesting fact: While Nelson was in prison he was offered freedom if he would help stop the violent actions of the ANC. He refused this offer.

Former South African President Mandela attends an African National Congress (ANC) election rally in Johannesburg before the 2009 elections.

Life in politics

After the 1948 election victory by the National Party, who supported apartheid, Mandela became actively involved in politics and the rights of black people in South Africa. Apartheid is an African word meaning 'separation' or 'apartness'. It is the name that South Africa's white government from 1948–1990 used to describe its discrimination against the country's non-white majority. Black people were denied a proper education, forced to live in specific areas away from white people and only allowed to do certain jobs.

> **" I detest racialism... whether it comes from a black man or a white man. "**
>
> Nelson Mandela

Nelson Mandela and his then wife Winnie salute the cheering crowds following his release from Victor Verster prison in February 1990.

In prison

In 1961, Mandela became leader of Umkhonto we Sizwe (meaning 'Spear of the Nation'), the armed wing of the ANC. He coordinated sabotage campaigns against military and government targets. In 1962, he was arrested and sentenced to life in prison. Mandela served most of his sentence on Robben Island. Prisoners were separated by colour, with black prisoners receiving the fewest rations.

Walk to freedom

Eventually, South African President FW de Klerk agreed to release Mandela from prison in 1990. Mandela was immediately elected President of the ANC and he and de Klerk worked together to bring apartheid to a peaceful end and to organise the country's first multi-racial elections. The ANC won and Mandela became the country's President.
He retired from politics in 1999, and worked tirelessly for several human rights organisations until his death.

MAKING HISTORY

For his commitment to bringing apartheid to an end and for his leadership of the ANC after his release from prison, Nelson Mandela was jointly awarded the Nobel Peace Prize in 1993 together with President FW de Klerk.

Kenneth Kaunda
Fighter for African Independence

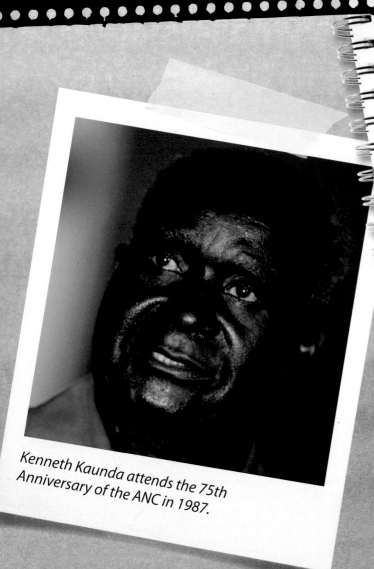

Kenneth Kaunda attends the 75th Anniversary of the ANC in 1987.

Name: Kenneth David Kaunda

Born: 28 April 1924, Chinsali, Northern Rhodesia (now Zambia)

Position: First President of Zambia 1964–1991

Awards and achievements: Brought independence to Zambia and campaigned against apartheid across Africa.

Interesting fact: From 2002 to 2008, Kaunda was the African President in Residence at Boston University, USA.

Independence for Zambia

Kaunda was jailed several times for distributing subversive (anti-government) literature and for being the leader of the banned Zambian African National Congress (ZANC). But rather than give up, he worked even harder to reach his goal of independence for all African countries.

Early life

Kenneth Kaunda was the youngest of eight children and grew up in Northern Rhodesia, a British colony that was ruled by a minority white government. As a young man, Kaunda worked as a teacher, a soldier and even a miner before devoting his life to the struggle for African independence.

While Kaunda was in prison, fellow ZANC members formed the United National Independence Party (UNIP). When Kaunda was released in 1960 he was elected president of UNIP and in January 1964, when UNIP won the country's election, Kaunda became Prime Minister.

Kenneth Kaunda was a strong and fearless leader who led his country to independence.

Zambia's leader

In October 1964, the country gained independence and took the name Zambia, from the Zambezi river, which runs through the country. Kaunda became the first President of Zambia and began the task of building a new country, investing in primary education and fighting to take back control of the country's important mineral rights, especially copper, from foreign companies like the British South Africa Company (BSAC).

African legacy

President Kaunda's opposition to white governments in Rhodesia (now Zimbabwe), South Africa and South-west Africa (now Namibia) meant that Zambia was often attacked by foreign rebel forces. The economy also suffered from falling world copper prices and is still one of the poorest countries in the world today. Kaunda's lasting legacy was in bringing independence to Zambia. Since retiring from office in 1991, he has devoted his life to fighting HIV and AIDS in Africa.

MAKING HISTORY

Kenneth Kaunda was an early fighter for African democracy. Nelson Mandela believed that Kaunda and Zambia were very important role models when he became President of South Africa. Mandela was able to learn from Zambia's developing democracy – what they did right and what they did wrong – to help South Africa emerge from its own white minority rule.

Shirley Chisholm
The Educator

Name: Shirley Anita St Hill Chisholm

Born: 30 November 1924, Brooklyn, New York, USA

Died: 1 January 2005

Position: US congresswoman 1969-83

Awards and achievements: The first African American woman elected to Congress.

Interesting fact: Shirley has had songs written about her by rappers Outkast and Method Man.

Shirley Chisholm addresses a crowd on the subject of racism in the Armed Forces in 1971.

Getting an education

Shirley Chisholm was born in New York City, USA to West Indian parents. She was sent to live with her grandmother in Barbados from the ages of 3–10, because her parents believed that the American education system was inadequate and they wanted their daughter to benefit from a traditional, British-style education. Chisholm returned to New York in 1934 and often credited those years in Barbados as the foundation of her success.

Working life

In 1946, Chisholm took a degree at Brooklyn College and then earned an MA in elementary education at Columbia University in 1952. From 1953–59 Chisholm worked as director of Hamilton-Madison Child Care Center, then as a consultant for local government from 1959–64.

> **"** I've always met more discrimination being a woman than being black. **"**
>
> *Shirley Chisholm*

In office

New York City in the 1950s and 1960s struggled to provide access to good education and services for its poorest residents. Working in education and child care for 14 years, Chisholm wanted to address these problems and this led her to run for a seat in the US Congress. In 1968, she was elected to represent New York's twelfth Congressional District. She supported employment and education programmes and the expansion of day care so that parents could afford to return to work.

Running for President

In 1972, Chisholm became the first woman to run for the Democratic Party Presidential nomination and the first black candidate of a major party to stand for President. She campaigned in 12 states and received 152 first-ballot votes but failed to beat fellow candidate George McGovern. Nevertheless, she was a ground-breaking politician whose influence can still be felt today.

Shirley Chisholm announces her intention to run for the Democratic Party Presidential nomination in Brooklyn, 1972.

MAKING HISTORY

Shirley Chisholm fought for freedom and equality in education and in the workplace. During her time in office, every colleague she hired for her congressional team was a woman and half of them were black.

Kofi Annan
The World's Peacemaker

An inspiring past

Annan's father was a noble of the Fante tribe in Ghana and his uncle and both of his grandfathers were tribal chiefs. The young Annan was sent to a Methodist boarding school from 1954–57, where he says he learned 'that suffering anywhere concerns people everywhere'.

Names: Kofi Atta Annan

Born: 8 April 1938, Kumasi, Gold Coast, Ghana

Position: Secretary-General of the United Nations 1997–2006

Awards and achievements: Joint winner of 2001 Nobel Peace Prize.

Interesting fact: In Ghana, children are named after the day of the week on which they are born. 'Kofi' means 'Friday'.

Kofi Annan has spent his life campaigning for peace throughout the world.

Education

Kofi Annan began a degree in economics in Ghana, then received a scholarship from the Ford Foundation that allowed him to complete his studies in the USA. Annan then took a degree in International Relations in Geneva, Switzerland.

66 We may have different religions, different languages, different coloured skin, but we all belong to one human race. 99

Kofi Annan

UN career

Annan worked for the UN as Assistant Secretary-General in three different areas. One of his biggest regrets was not being able to stop the Rwandan genocide in 1994, when members of the majority Hutu tribe turned on the minority ruling Tutsi tribe, killing an estimated 800,000 people over the course of 100 days. He swore that in future he would do everything in his power to persuade the world to act more quickly to prevent the loss of innocent lives.

MAKING HISTORY

When the United Nations was formed in 1945, the position of Secretary-General was described by US President Roosevelt as a 'world moderator' – someone who would speak out and play an important role in keeping world peace. As the UN grew to its current 192 member countries, the Secretary-General's role now includes a large number of global issues. Kofi Annan was influential in raising the profile of the job in the eyes of the world. He persuaded member countries that they had a responsibility to the world as a whole and not just to their own nations.

Position of power

As Secretary-General, Annan was persuasive and compassionate. He saw his responsibility as acting as the world's conscience. He used UN troops to try and stop fighting everywhere from Kosovo to Darfur. He raised funds and awareness to reduce the spread of AIDS, combat diabetes and increase the rights of women.

Kofi Annan is decorated with the Dominican Republic's Order of Duarte, Sanchez and Mella in 2006. It is the country's highest honour and is given for distinguished services.

Ellen Johnson-Sirleaf
First Woman President

A good beginning

Ellen Johnson-Sirleaf's parents were both from prominent Liberian families who pushed their daughter to develop an international outlook. She studied economics at the college of West Africa from 1948–55 and then travelled to the US in 1961 to continue her studies, eventually earning a degree at the University of Colorado, USA. She followed that with two years at Harvard University, USA (1969–71), where she earned an MA in economics and public policy.

Name: Ellen Johnson-Sirleaf

Born: 29 October 1938, Monrovia, Liberia

Position: President of Liberia 2006-present

Awards and achievements: The only elected female head of state in Africa.

Interesting fact: Ellen's story was told in the 2008 documentary entitled *Pray the Devil Back to Hell.*

As President, Sirleaf is working to improve social conditions and has made education free and compulsory for all junior school children.

Sirleaf returned to Liberia to work as Assistant Minister of Finance from 1972–73 and then Minister of Finance from 1979–80. In 1980, the government was overthrown by military leaders and the President and several cabinet members were shot. Sirleaf escaped to Kenya and then to the USA.

Becoming President

The military coup led to two civil wars that devastated Liberia's economy and killed thousands of people. When a peace treaty was signed in 2003 between the government and rebel groups, Sirleaf returned to Liberia and eventually won the presidential election in 2005.

Condoleezza Rice
The Special Advisor

A concert dream

Condoleezza Rice was born into a family where education, music and the arts were extremely important. Her father was a minister and her mother taught music and public speaking. Rice started learning French, music and ballet at three years old. At 15, she began taking lessons to be a concert pianist but decided to focus on her education because she felt she did not have the ability to be a professional musician.

Studies

Rice was a high academic achiever. She finished her degree in political science at 19 and earned a PhD at just 26. As soon as she completed her PhD in 1981, she was hired by Stanford University as a Professor of Political Science. She was a specialist on the Soviet Union and one of her lectures in 1985 caught the attention of US National Security Advisor Brent Scowcroft.

Moving into politics

When George W Bush became President in 1989, Scowcroft brought Rice to the White House to help develop US government policy towards the Soviet Union. She returned to Stanford to teach in 1991 but maintained her political connections, taking a one-year leave of absence to help with Bush's 2000 presidential campaign.

Name: Condoleezza Rice

Born: 14 November 1954, Birmingham, Alabama, USA

Position: US National Security Advisor 2001-2005, US Secretary of State 2005-2009

Awards and achievements: First African American woman US Secretary of State.

Interesting fact: Her name comes from the Italian musical expression 'con dolcezza' meaning 'with sweetness'.

After two spells in US government, Condoleezza Rice is again working at Stanford University as a political science professor.

Barack Obama
The First Black US President

Name: Barack Hussein Obama II

Born: 4 August 1961, Honolulu, Hawaii, USA

Position: The 44th President of the United States 2009–present

Awards and achievements: Winner of 2009 Nobel Peace Prize and *Time* Magazine's Person of the Year 2008.

Interesting fact: Barack won a Grammy Award in 2006 for Best Spoken Word Recording for the audio version of his autobiography *Dreams from My Father*.

Barack Obama taught constitutional law at the University of Chicago Law School from 1992–2004, before being elected to the US Senate.

> " There is not a black America and a white America... there's the United States of America. "
>
> *Barack Obama*

The early years

Barack Obama was born in Hawaii to a white American mother and a black Kenyan father. His parents divorced in 1964, when Obama Senior left Hawaii to study at Harvard University. His mother remarried Indonesian student Lolo Soetoro and the family moved to Jakarta, Indonesia. Obama lived there from 1967–71, before returning to live with his maternal grandparents in Hawaii to attend senior school.

As the first black president of a traditionally white publication, Obama started to gain national media attention. He was offered a publishing contract to write a book on race relations that became his best-selling autobiography *Dreams from My Father*, published in 1995.

Becoming President

Obama's personal beliefs have always been to help people maximise their personal freedoms – the right to vote, the right to housing, the right to earn a living and the right to healthcare. These commitments have been constant through the time he was elected to the Illinois Senate in 1996, to the US Senate in 2004 and most of all when he was elected US President in November 2008.

President Obama's abilities as an inspirational public speaker helped win his election campaign.

Studying hard

Obama was always very ambitious and hard-working. He won a place at the prestigious Columbia University to study political science and, after graduating, worked in community housing projects in Chicago, before attending Harvard Law School. At Harvard, he was elected president of the *Law Review*, a long-standing and well-respected journal dating back to the nineteenth century that was published by Harvard students.

MAKING HISTORY

As President, Barack Obama has passed a number of important and historic laws. To combat global recession, he passed The American Recovery and Reinvestment Act (2009), pumping $787 billion (£520 billion) into the US economy. Perhaps most important though, is the Affordable Healthcare for America Act (2009), which for the first time gave 36 million Americans the right to free and subsidised healthcare.

Other Rulers and Leaders

Baroness Valerie Ann Amos (1954-)

Baroness Amos was leader of the UK House of Lords from 2003–2007. Born in Guyana and educated in England, Valerie became Chief Executive of the Equal Opportunities Commission in 1989, advising the South African government on human rights and employment law. As leader of the House of Lords, she often spoke out about international development and foreign affairs.

Kwame Nkrumah (1909–1972)

Kwame was the leader of Ghana and the Gold Coast from 1952 to 1966. He campaigned against British colonial rule in his country and spent time in prison for his actions. His Convention People's Party (CPP) won the country's first free election, making Kwame President. He modernised Ghana, helping it to become one of the wealthiest countries in Africa.

Colin Luther Powell (1937-)

The first African American US Secretary of State (2001–2005). Born in New York City to Jamaican immigrant parents, Powell was a professional soldier for 35 years. He was the Secretary of State in George W Bush's Administration and remains active in public and political life.

Dr Susan Elizabeth Rice (1964-)

Born in Washington DC, USA, Rice is the current US Ambassador to the United Nations. She won scholarships to Stanford University, then Oxford, where she studied history and international relations. Rice became Assistant Secretary of State for African Affairs in 1997 and worked to help Africa compete in the global economy. A foreign policy advisor to President Obama during his election campaign, Rice is the first African American woman US representative to the United Nations.

Julius Kambarage Nyerere (1922–1999)

He became Tanganyika's first Prime Minister in 1961 and President a year later when the country became a republic. Nyerere was instrumental in the birth of Tanzania, when the islands of Zanzibar united with mainland Tanganyika in 1964.

Jacob Gedleyihlekisa 'Msholozi' Zuma (1942-)

Zuma is the President of South Africa. He joined the ANC at 17 and was arrested in 1963 for conspiring to overthrow the apartheid government. Zuma spent ten years in prison, then lived in exile in Mozambique, returning to South Africa in 1990. Zuma became President of the ANC in 2007 and South African President two years later.

Timeline

Legacy

1624 Nzinga becomes Queen of Andongo

1776 Toussaint Louverture freed from slavery

1930 Haile Selassie crowned Emperor of Ethiopia

1957 Kwame Nkrumah becomes Prime Minister of Ghana

1964 Kenneth Kaunda becomes President of independent Zambia

1964 Julius Nyerere becomes first President of Tanzania

1968 Shirley Chisholm becomes the first black woman elected to US Congress

1994 Nelson Mandela becomes South Africa's first black President

2000 Condoleezza Rice named US National Security Advisor

2001 Kofi Annan and the United Nations receive the Nobel Peace Prize

2001 Colin Powell becomes the first African American US Secretary of State

2003 Baroness Amos becomes Leader of the House of Lords

2005 Ellen Johnson-Sirleaf becomes Africa's first female President

2008 Barack Obama is elected President of the United States of America

2009 Jacob Zuma becomes President of South Africa

2009 Barack Obama is sworn in as the first African American President of the US

2009 Susan Rice becomes US Ambassador to the United Nations

2013 Barack Obama sworn in for a second Presidential term after being re-elected

The legacies of the rulers and leaders in this book live on, not only in their achievements but also through the work of their families and followers:

The Nelson Mandela Foundation www.nelsonmandela.org/ index.php
Mandela established the Foundation after he retired as President of South Africa. The Foundation focuses on spreading peace and unity.

The Global Fund www.theglobalfund.org/en
Kofi Annan founded this charity to fight AIDS, tuberculosis (TB) and malaria. It is the world's largest funder of programs to combat TB and malaria, and provides 20 per cent of world funding to combat AIDS.

The Kenneth Kaunda Children of Africa Foundation http://www.facebook.com/ group.php?gid=87179224121
Set up to fight the AIDS epidemic in Africa and to help the children orphaned by the disease.

Glossary

Index

Abolish To do away with or end.

Apartheid The South African National Party's official government policy of racial separation, or 'segregation', from 1948–1990.

Coloniser A person who settles in a country a long way from their own homeland, but maintains ties with it.

Constitution The rules or principles on which a country is governed or ruled.

Correspondence course A method of studying by post. Teachers send out work assignments and students send back their essays for marking.

Democratic For the benefit of everyone.

Democratically elected A government or leader who is chosen to lead a country or group based on a system of voting that allows everyone a vote.

Economic reform Improvements or changes to the economy of a country, for example how the wealth is divided between rich and poor.

Exile A prolonged, usually enforced, absence from one's home or country.

Founder member One of the first or original members who helps to set up or establish an organisation.

Guerrilla troops A part-time, politically motivated, armed force that fights against stronger regular forces.

Majority A group that is different racially or politically, for example, from a smaller group of which it is a part.

Minority A group that is different racially or politically, for example, from a larger group of which it is a part.

Peace treaty An agreement to end a war or conflict.

Plantation A large farm or estate where crops such as rubber or sugar cane are grown.

Racial discrimination The unfair treatment of a person or racial group based on prejudice.

Republic A form of government in which the people or their elected representatives hold power.

Revolution The overthrow of a government or political system by the people.

Segregation To set apart from a main group.